FROM MY HEART

FROM MY HEART

❖ VOLUME I ❖

By
SHIRLEY JONES WITCHER

Published by Mill City Press

Mill City Press, Inc.
212 3rd Avenue North, Suite 570
Minneapolis, MN 55401
612.455.2294
www.millcitypress.net

ISBN - 1-934937-13-4
ISBN - 978-1-934937-13-6
LCCN - 2008930013

Cover Design by Ana Loscin
Typeset by Philippe Duquesnoy

Printed in the United States of America

CONTENTS PAGE

I dedicate this book "FROM MY HEART"
to my three successful and prosperous sons:
Jason, Timothy and Jeremy.
To my first grandchild, Janiya;
one with much knowledge and wisdom;
to my grandson; Justice,
who will one day become a mighty, strong man of God.
Jared-the one who will have a strong voice
to speak the Word of God in season and out of season;
to Amani; the one who will be active and joyous for God;
her voice will bring a message to the world.
Julius, who will have great insight, wisdom and discernment.
To all future grandchildren, and great grandchildren;
I know you will be the ones God will also use to reach many hurting
people; this book I dedicate to you also.

"FROM THE HEART"
will always be available for your reading.
I will also record this book
for your hearing so that you will always
be able to hear my voice anytime of the day

Mom-Grandma will always love you;
keeping you close to my heart.

May the Blessings of God always be upon you
and your children
and your children's children.

MEMORIES FOREVER GONE

All the good memories are here to
Star; never will they go away-they
are forever embedded in my heart;
my mind and part of my soul.

I release all the bad memories
from my mind and will forgive
myself of all the mistakes I made
in time.

The good memories will never go
away-they are here to stay embedded
in my heart, my mind and my soul.

Don't be afraid to let go even though
it hurts so' to let go of all the disasters
that has taken place. Just say, memories
forever gone of all those wrongs and
remember the good things that must come.

We don't have long to enjoy life's pleasures
we cannot even measure the length of
time. Now just let go forever all of the
memories that have kept you in bondage.

Memories forever gone-the past of all the
wrongs

GOOD MEMORIES COME TODAY.

MY BEST FRIEND

I cherish you.
I appreciate you.
I love you.
You are my best friend.

The years go by-we cried,
laughed, shared and
compared the things that
were going on.

Thirty-seven years of trust;
our connection was a must-
as we walked sometimes
arm and arm-hand and hand.
We are like twins forever
connected; mind and spirit;
no one can come between us
You are my best friend.

I miss talking with you and
getting your advice on matters
I shared with no other; laughing,
sharing, crying and praying. I
want to believe that those days
are not gone forever. I miss you.
You are my best friend.

Your being in pain from cancer
is hard to explain; on the inside
you are still the same. I miss sharing
the Word of God with you; whereby
we draw our strength together.

We are strong in the faith and we know
God cares, but the pain in my heart is
almost too much to share with anyone.

I pray that you will rise up and conquer
this disease; but if not; always remember

YOU ARE MY BEST FRIEND.

WHAT TIME IS IT

Do you know what time it is?
Your time might be morning
or day-evening or midnight;
no one can say.

Why, because time is different
and has its own destiny. You
have to seek and find for your-
self the time to make that
move in the right direction.

Our minds and ourselves, at times
don't know, so we seek God's
counsel to make sure that the
time is right for sure. The right
time is precious.

Many decisions and changes
come-you have to know what
time to go and take that step
that will allow you to move forward;
to succeed, to accomplish what has
to be for you to do what you should
do-Now Today-Tomorrow-that is
definitely you.

WHAT TIME IS IT FOR YOU.

FIGHT TO WIN

Even though it seems as if I have
lost-I have not-I am not a loser-I
will always win.

Is it hard to give all your energy-your
mind racing of thoughts of how to
succeed-it is worth it-to fight to
win.

The negative thoughts keep on
comparing what others have done-
but I have to challenge everyone
to let them know I am capable of
being someone GREAT.

This race I fight is not really hard
because I know that in the end-I
WIN. Don't give up-continue to
challenge yourself of those many
dreams; that talent; that goal that
lives inside of you.

FIGHT TO WIN

FIGHT ON.

RESPECT YOURSELF

If you don't respect yourself-you
have know right to expect someone
else to respect you.

You don't think you need to do
something to succeed. Your walk,
your talk, your attitude reveals to
others that you don't care-You just
don't Respect Yourself.

You blame your mother, father too;
your teachers and principals that want
to help you-succeed.

What do you do? Reject the ones that
are willing to help you; the ones God has
put in your path to achieve, to advance
and be all that life created you to do.

Now what-you stand on the corner; lost,
blind; don't want to see or realize that
your life is just about over.

Examine your mind-now look at yourself
on that corner doing nothing-hanging out
with the wrong friends; doing nothing to
make accomplishments.

Now decide what you want to do-take
that first step and start afresh-go back to
school; get a career and don't look back
of life's mess that was once there.

No, you are more than that-not respecting others because you don't respect yourself.

Now, what are you going to do?

RESPECT YOURSELF-OTHERS WILL RESPECT YOU.

DON'T GROW UP

Time passes by, oh to quickly;
My child, my child is all grown up.

I miss all the noise of children
playing, laughing and saying:

WHEN IS IT TIME TO EAT?

I miss assuring my sons, and
their friends too, helping them
decide what to do. I shared with
them that life has many knocks-
some good-some bad; no matter
what takes place, be glad that you
are able to overcome-why, because
you are more than a conqueror.

In my mind-I say don't grow up-but
I know in my heart that day will come;
has already begun. They are on their
own now watching their children play,
laugh and saying;

WHEN IS IT TIME TO EAT?

Their parents say in their mind, what
joy this child brings us each day-our
lives have just begun.

In their heart, they know that one day
that child will grow up; then each child
will say, as they look back one day;

HOW DID I GROW UP SO FAST.

LIVING

Ha, Ha, Ha
are you kidding-?
The life you are
living; is it for real?
Are you happy still?

What satisfies you
no longer satisfies me-I'm
free-I'm living.

The same things everyday;
washing, shopping, cooking,
cleaning too; bathing the
children; taking them to school;
activities, play, schoolwork each
day; No break today; Is that
really living.

At that time, it was the greatest
joy of all to watch my three sons
grow and stand tall; accomplishing
what is important in life-That was
living.

Now, my life has totally changed-
or is it really the same; all these
memories still live inside of me.

HA, HA, HA-I RELIVE-LIVE-AND AM LIVING.

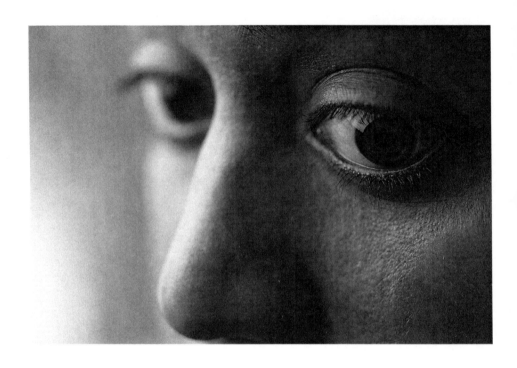

AFRAID

Why are you afraid to go out and
discover the world that can offer you
so very much.

You panic, you draw back, you say
I'm not good enough?
Who told you that? You were born
with a destiny. You can be great; do
do extraordinary things; explore the
world with no fear in place.

Because you have been wonderfully
Made; no one can make you
afraid to doubt what God has made;
beautifully made.

God has made you; now stop.

NO LONGER BE AFRAID.

DON'T STOP

Why are you stopping now? You just
begun to see-to know-what you can do.

Why are you stopping now?-They don't
believe that you can do it. Your mind is
full, so full of all these accomplishments
that must come forth-don't entertain
those negative thoughts. I know you
hear those critics say don't you dear
explore those things today; but your mind
keeps saying to you-Why are you
stopping?-this is what you do-
Close your ears to those who don't
care about your accomplishments.

Don't Stop Here
Don't Stop Now
Don't Stop At All
Don't Ever Stop Again

Your Time Has Just Begun

DON'T STOP.

TOGETHER

Line up and see
One by One
Two by Two
side by side
Revive-Strength;
YOU ARE ALIVE.

You are lined up;
Next to One
Next to Two
Side by Side

The strength, the binding
of you-will never separate
what you can do. Sometimes
it takes one or two to stand
side by side-to watch and
encourage you to do-all that
is meant for you-TO DO.

Now, arise-stay in line-one
by one-two by two-side by
side and you will know exactly
what is purposed for you.
All of your hopes and dreams
are true-now your mind is alive
today to stay in line.

ONE BY ONE
TWO BY TWO.

YOUR BIRTH

Born to be free; you must
earn the degree of lives
experiences-Birth

The first breath you take
comes life; birth comes from
the experiences of life after
you are born.

Your inner self is only born
when you connect to birth
which comes from the creator.

For birth to be born only comes-
when-where-the existence of
yourself becomes aware that
birth is not freedom. Born, only
will be where life exists deep
inside of thee-through life
experiences; then you are born
conquering all;

Failures-Success; Success-
Failures-Now you are born;

NOW YOU KNOW BIRTH.

RESTORATION

Oh How I long to be like I use to be;
Oh, how I long to live again;
So full of life.

I long to see the sun rise and the
Moon set in my life; my laughter
was fresh, bursting with energy
overflowing.

Oh how I long to live again to touch,
to feel, to hear clearly the people
I love, the beauty of life that surrounds
me.

Oh How I long to live again.
Now I feel sadness; I feel the pain
of death; I see blood all around me.
I hear the sounds of a blast; I see
holes in his head; I see fear upon his
face; I see smoke and flames; I see
him no more; nothing is left for he was
burned to death beyond recognition,
nothing was left.

Nothing is left, inside I die the same
kind of death. I can't touch or feel or
hear.

Oh how I long to live again.

RESTORATION

MY SON

Legos,
blocks,
trains, cars and planes,
paint, puzzles and clay;
my son and me.

We drew together
closeness forever
as we touched each other
and wanted one another to
enjoy playing.

I see in my mind
the kinds of fun we had
through tired nights and
many days; I'm glad I
took the time to play;
blocks, Legos, cars and
trains.

I'll never forget the smile on
his face when the blocks did
not fall down. Even though
it could not stay this way-I'll
never forget how much we played.

Paint on our hands and on our
face; some spreading across the
floor and table too.

It didn't matter because we were
together loving one another-forever-
nothing can take the place of this
picture in my mind.

I'll never forget
How much it meant to have

MY SON

WHAT'S GOING ON

You don't know
You can't know
Conceive-perceive-deceive
what's going on inside
of m?

You pretend to know
Oh, but you don't understand
the depths of my mind-I can
see right through you.

You try to share
the pain I share; my
inner self. Do you really care?
Or want to share my thoughts-
my feelings-I will not open up
no more-for the wounds of my
soul must heal.

Will I let you in again? No I
don't think so-see-you don't
see what's going on inside of me;
You really don't care to know.

It's all right because I know I'm
right to feel this way-it's sad to
know-you don't know what's going
on inside of me.

You can't even conceive-you deceive-
but it's all right-I know what's going on.

You won't know-you will go; no longer
will you be a part of me-my life, my plans, my dreams

Only God and me
He knows what's inside of me

NOW MOVE ON

SLEEP LITTLE CHILD

The child inside of me won't sleep;
she plays and plays-singing, dancing,
and jumping rope.

But, you are a woman now-this child
keeps rising up inside of me.

She makes me laugh-I can't sleep
tonight-I want to play inside my mind-
singing, dancing, and jumping rope again.

Don't sleep my child; wake up to a
life full of expectancy-dreams-see-
you can put this behind-this childlike
thinking of the mind.

Grow up now-fight and see, what life
really offers thee; sleep little child;
don't rise again-life begins;

I'M AWAKE-I AM AWAKE

LAUGHTER COME OUT

Hidden behind that mind of sorrow-what's
dying to come out?-Laughter.

You want to smile, jump for joy, sing
and laugh. Where are you-I look and
search my mind, my heart-I can hear you
deep inside of me-come forth Laughter-I
know you can be a part of my life again.

The things called sorrow, hurt, loneliness,
despair is eating inside my mind and
distracts the peace that lies deep inside
of me,

What do I do now-I push in to push out-
push out- and push in continually. This time
laughter will come on the inside of me;
radiates on the outside for the world to
see;

LAUGHTER you will never go away-again

THEY USE ME

Understand-I Win-No matter what-
life begins anew-afresh in me.

I can't say why they take advantage
of me-they say I'm weak but I am
strong to know what has gone wrong.

They used me-abused me-but I don't
care-really I know what I can bare; I
will share with you one day-the pain-
\what, the pain, the pain that won't go
away; It will one day-not today-It will
one day; now-you can't use me no
more. I have opened up that door-I
let you out.

Hold back my love because of what
you did-NEVER-I will live a life of
victory-full of love for you-for me.

Don't you know the world needs a
person like me. I no longer exist-I
exist to live-a life full of love

YOU CAN'T USE ME NO MORE

YOU DON'T CARE

You Don't Care

Your thoughts, your words
come at me-
You say you do;

You womanize you fantasize;
I am not included-you do it-
you do what you want to;

You Don't Care
You say you do.

You curse-you rehearse
to tear down my walls of
security-independency-you
go as if nothing happened
TO ME.

I smile-you smile back
knowing that you lack the
love you can give me.
It's too late-go away
to your place of hiding.

I am going to stay and find
my place of rest and security;
It lies within me.

I care-you don't even though
you say you do.

Go away-let life come here-
to me- a life of peace-security.

No rest will come to thee

YOU DON'T CARE

THE LIGHTS GO OFF

Darkness comes in-lingering there-where
inside of me? Why-The lights go off.
I will come again-when I allow myself
to see that I must pull that string in my mind;
to be all that God has for me-

The Lights Go Off-
A new day begins-over-over
again-in my mind-in my mind-
It goes out the door-destitute; empty;
despondent; I feel the darkness that
instills my life; The lights go off-come
back on so I can see-
WHERE AM I GOING?

In my mind I run to see the brightness
of the sun awaiting, awaiting to
rescue me from the pressure of
my mind that's causing this darkness
to rise-
WHERE AM I GOING?

You see-now I see the light inside
of me-pushing-pushing out of me;

Be Free to Shine with the world-

The lights go off
The lights come on.

LIVE AGAIN-YOU CAN

FLASHBACKS

The sound is so vivid to me-
sirens all around me-
lights flashing-horns blowing-
people passing by me;
I see, I hear, I know that
they are there-what are they
waiting for.
RESCUE ME

I lie in this deep hole-
no one sees-or hears me
screaming down here
in this dark hole
Come, RESCUE ME

My breathing gets lighter-
I seem to fade away-but
deep in my mind I stay-
to live-to hear these sirens
within-don't you hear me
crying out to you?
Come, RESCUE ME

Time is running out
they go away-not finding
me today. This way laying
hopelessly, helplessly, again
today. In this pit of despair;
waiting-hoping to be fixed.

Nope-no one comes to Rescue
Me-but here I lie-victoriously-
For me Today-I AM FREE

SUN-SHINE-SUNSHINE

Do you really want to see
What God has for thee.

Do you want to sit in your
place of defeat; wondering

Get Up! Don't you Know
The sun will shine again?
Sunshine

Don't be like that-don't let
depression take a hold of thee;
Get up now-see what's around
the corner-can't you see;
Dreams that will come to be.

Can't you see-the sun-shine-
sunshine-inside of you-Come
Out Now-Don't, Won't, Stay
Inside of Me

Reach up-Reach out-No Doubt;
the things that God has ordained
for thee-Now; Right Now-The
Sun-Shine-Sunshine-Is, will,
must come again.

Go inside now; take hold;
Don't ever let go; Sun-Shine-Sunshine Within

RISE-RISE AGAIN

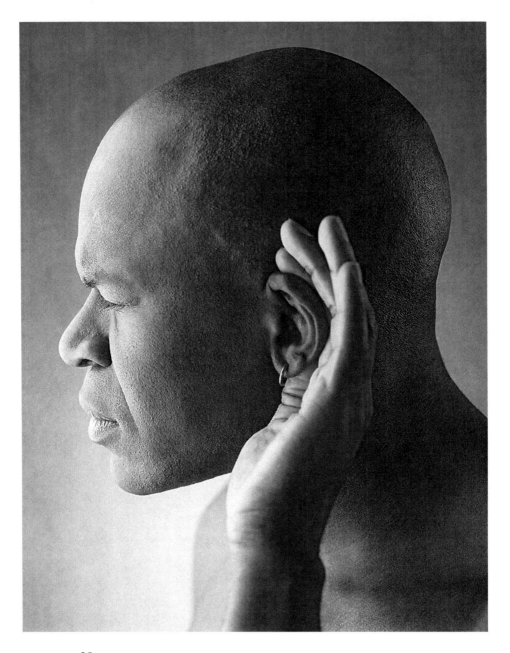

I HEAR YOU

This voice inside of me- I hear you-what
did you say?-Come with me-you will see,
listen, perceive from this voice that I
share-to gain-to profit to remain forever
in me-I'm not ashamed. I hear you;
You're always there-what-speak loud
and clear-to my mind-to my soul;
whatever it is that grows; that which will
help me reach my goal.

Who knows what it is-I hear this voice
ringing that which my spirit brings;
Come with me-come inside of me to
hear what God is saying to me.

Succeed-Succeed-you have no need-to clamor
up-close up-shut up. No you will not shut
this door no more to this voice that cries
within.

I Hear You

I Hear You

Now, what do I do-
Listen to what you have to say, follow
all your instructions given to you today.

Life Begins Now
Now Life Begins
For I Listen to the voice within

Hush Now
Listen Now
Rest Now
Hear Your Voice Speaking

WHISPER

Whisper into my ear-what do you hear-
the voices screaming out in fear-inside
of me.

Whisper into my ear-The words of hope;
no despair-no more loud sounds of
hopelessness here-the clinging sounds
of doubt and fear-ringing again and again
in my inner ear. Don't whisper these
lifeless screams-hollering inside of me;
No more will your voice stick inside of my
mind, causing me to have fear-life can
bring much more than that-to me.

Whisper into my ear-cry out to me; live,
live again-rejoice; for I know that
deep within me life begins for me -Again.

Whisper Hope
Whisper Love
Whisper All The Things God Gives From Above.

Darkness and Death
No longer take hold-of me-Never Again;
Whisper In My Ear The sound of a voice
that really cares-A voice from above;
God Really Cares For Me.

He whispers LIFE-HOPE-HOPE-MORE HOPE

LIFE

HOLD ME PLEASE

I lay my head under the rib cage of your bosom.
Next to your heart-I feel your warmth-your heart
beat-ecstasy-ecstasy-love flowing from thee;
the warmth of you.

Hold me Lord Please-Majesty. Only you can
hold me-to please me like no other-God of Love;
majesty.

Peace comes from you to me this night.
Brightness I see-injected-projected-inside,
around-all about me.

Hold me please Lord-Hold Me. The fire that
burns within me-inside of me comes from your
warmth-I lay my head under your rib cage.

Tears no more-this night take flight-Peace
comes again---

I SLEEP

COME WITH ME

Come on let's take a journey of the mind-
every fiber of your being tells you to take
a deep journey-look deep inside that mind
of yours-A seed has been planted in the
womb of that woman-that girl-who watches;
yet grows to maturity.

Can't, won't, don't want to know where to
go-but watch, you will see me, that seed
that has been planted deep within my mind;
grow to maturity.

Where do I go from here-don't you want to
know-I care that some day you will share
with me how far this seed that is planted
within me-yet grows to maturity Wait and see
Now-Come Take This Journey With Me.

WHERE DO I GO

Where do I go?-can you see that I am so very far
from thee.

You can't find me-but I really don't care-for I
am searching for me-so far away from you-so far from myself.

As I walk-as I hide from the pressures of my
mind-I search, whatever
is hiding deep inside of me.

Where do I go-do I sit and wait-or run to find
what's inside of my mind.

It's so deep, too deep, far too deep for me
to keep searching-the inner thoughts of my
mind.

NOW---WHERE DO I GO FROM HERE

RUN

Run, Leap, Jump-whatever it takes-run
for your life-escape from the fear, the
darkness that surrounds you is near-
jump, jump high over the struggles of

life-the pain, the shame-run to escape;
you must gain all that belongs to you;
look. it is the highest peak-reach and
grab hold-never let go-there is an
opening for me, for you-to share-your
goals-your dreams-future-success
comes to me-to you.

Use all your strength-breath-breath
the air within-then life will come again.
You will see-each step you take-each jump
you make-you will see me running
towards my goal.

RUN-TAKE A BREATH-

RUN-TO YOUR PLACE-REST-PEACE

TRUST ME

My heart aches, the tears fall, a dry spell
is here, but one day soon, O Lord, you will
wipe every tear away.

For you promised in your Word that no
more tears will be-so you say rejoice my
daughter for I am I am with thee-I am
here-I see-trust me.

The world will see how I will remove every
stumbling block from thee and the blessings
that are flowing from me.

Trust me and know that you will grow and
stand strong for the world to see-for I am
here and you must know that I am blessing
thee.

TRUST ME

TODAY IS THE DAY

Today is the day that you will shine your
glorious light down upon me.
Today is the day of deliverance for me.

I will not go back to once was-for you
have set my life totally free.

Today is the day, Lord, that I will rejoice
in you and praise you forever afresh and
new.

For I have discovered something special
today-I know within my heart and I can
hear you say-

Today is the day I have set you totally

FREE

LET ME FIND MYSELF IN YOU

O God of the universe, will I forever praise
thee; in times like these you are forever there.

Though I do not see thee, I feel your loving
arms around me-

O God of the universe you are forever there.

Grant me, what I have asked of you, for my
heart is here to please you-My God of the
Universe.

Your word is truth-a comfort-my place to
hide, search-for I long to be close to you-nearer
to you as I find myself.

How I long to please you. When, how-help me
to find my place in you Lord; my God of mercy
and hope.

Take time out for me today Lord and hear my cry
I plead to thee.

Search my heart and if you find what's not suppose
to be-Dear Lord remove it from me, I pray.

I need an answer today Lord-my heart will fail me
if I continue to wait.

Take time out for me today Lord-Hear my cry
today.

SPEAK OUT

I'm Free-I can say what's inside of me-Don't
stop me now-Don't even try to throw my words
into the sea to drown me out-I shall speak out.

Who do you think you are?-I said I am free to
Speak from my heart what is inside of me.

Some words may not fall on good soil to you,
But every word I speak is surly true.

I'm free-God has set me free to speak out-
To help set others free.

Now look at me-don't you see that I am free
For whom the son has set free, is free indeed.

You must see that the only way to be free

SPEAK OUT WITH A LOUD VOICE TO BE
HEARD -SPEAK OUT SPEAK OUT

PICK UP-MOVE ON

Pick up-Move On
Get Over It-
That's Life.

Laughter-Tears
No more fears;
That's Life.

Stop Complaining-Anticipating
know that you can pick up
and move on-expand and see
what's out there for thee.

So what-they hurt you
talked about you-kicked
you to the ground-
Just get up-pickup-move on.

Now they can see just what
you can be-You don't need them
to hinder thee; NO MORE;
God's in your corner-that's all
that matters.
Get Up-Pick Up-Keep moving on.

RELEASE-RELIEVED

Unlock that chain.
You have been locked
up too long.

RELEASE YOURSELF TODAY

Unlock that door.
Let it close no more.
It only hinders you
from achieving and
accomplishing every-
thing you can do. You
can do much much more.

RELEASE YOURSELF TODAY

Unlock your gate.
Let yourself see why
am I hiding myself from
this world for others to
see my accomplishments.
I have so much to offer.

RELEASE YOURSELF TODAY

Now, I take the key of
my mind and I say;
Release Me-now I am
relieved to know that I
am totally free.

RELEASE-RELIEVED

NO MORE

No more fear will be injected into my soul.
No more tears of fear-the sound of violence
ringing in my ear.

No more delight coming from your eyes-rage
of hate that lingers on inside of you-as you still
see my hurt.

No more will you sit back and watch the fear
that comes from me-you sit and look at me
with a sense of victory-you conqueror nothing
pain that shakes my soul-deep inside I will
WIN-OVER-AND OVER-AGAIN

No More

ENTRANCE

Enter inside of me Can you-Can
you see deep inside my soul; the
hurt, the pain-the joy, the peace
that keeps arising inside of me.

Enter in-look hard-not with your
mind-enter into my heart-your
heart must feel what's inside of me.
Will it go away? Someday you will
see-not with your mind, even though
the mind can set you free-only the
heart reveals what is really inside
of me.

Enter In-Enter Inside of me.

REACH OUT TO ME-PLEASE

I KNOW I CAN

I know I can-but do I really know what life has in store for me?

I know I can do all things through Christ, but do I
know what as been ordained for me?

I look deep inside but nothing seems to come forth
but within me is life; a life of dreams-a life that needs
to fulfill its entire destiny.

Only through Christ can this be done; He ordained
me and knows where I come from. Breast to Breast
I am connected to Him-I can and I will find the place
where I should be-It's not too late to grab hold of what
God has for mw.

I KNOW I CAN-I CAN-I KNOW I CAN

WHO AM I

Who Am I?
What do you see? I look at myself, I
look at you as who, as what, as a being
as a human being.

What is that? Mere flesh, what does it
consist of?. Do you rally know. From ash
to ash; dust to dust. The bones, the spirit,
the mind, the soul.

What Am I? Who are we; what are we made
of; what are we to be.

Look deep into my eyes; what do you see.
A being, a person-so deep you really cannot
see, but I am who I am-intelligent, warm, full
of joy. Sometimes happy, sometimes sad; meek
humble, compassionate at times; who controls
this mind? Who Am I?

Powerful, but yet not so; tall, but not so;
wanting to conquer many things, but not always
knowing how; strong, but yet weak.

Determined; but Am I; passing by, but yet still
here.

Doing much; but yet doing nothing.

Accomplishments must come, will come. A
conqueror, a warrior, I am?

Who Am I? Who are we? A Being-A Mere Being.

CLOUDS OF LIFE

Light-Blue
Dark-Gray
That's the colors of life.

Sunshine Anew
Darkness and Gloom

Rain falls
laughter Calls
clouds go away-for awhile
Sunshine stays-darkness
gloom lingers on-the moon
covers my light though the
sunshine is bright inside of
me.

Clouds go away
you want to stay
and run my life.
The light inside of me
elopes around me and
covers the clouds that
shapes-reshapes but
escapes.

Don't let the clouds stay
so long;
You come-you go-today
you must not control my
life.

strong and
determined
that I am.

I will shine again
even though I know
the clouds of life will
come-and go; again I will be

strong and
determined.

That I am.

TALK TO ME

I yearn, I desire, I dream, I wish, I hope
that-you-will-talk to me.

They wave at me, they look down at me,
to see, to examine, to watch, even smile,
that smile, that warmth, that glow that
touches my heart.

The tears fall like rain drops' but laughter
comes, shines like the sun.

I laugh, I smile, I look up at you, waiting,
yearning, growing weak, tired, hoping to
hear that special sound, those words, to
come-to speak out to me, at me--strong
words, soothing words.

You can't, oh; I wish you could, because
you are so elegant, full of life, full of
beauty-I thought you could, you would; I
waited for you to talk to me, but you are
a lovely tree-you cannot talk-you cannot
talk to me.

EXCITEMENT

HI; Hooray, Good day
I am so happy to say;
I'm fine, I'm great; Oh,
what a beautiful day.

Come with me, let's look
and find what makes me
so happy to see what each
day will bring.

Oh God, I am so grateful to
know that you have made me
to feel such beauty-you see only
because of you, the excitement
wells up inside of me to express
all that I feel today, Oh God, I
am so grateful to you.

Hi, Hooray, Good day, I am
Blessed.

Oh how excited I am to know
that I am excited about life

TODAY.

OPEN THE DOOR

Unlock the door of thoughts that surround my heart,
my emotions. So much love-deep, deep inside the
cavity, the wall that opens up, but yet stays closed.

Fear, uncertainty, determination, strength-love
Conquers all-the door opens-the door closes-the
door opens-shall I walk through the wall of my
heart-shall I leap, leap forward, high pass the
eyes of existence-or shall I hide behind the wall
that will disappear and no one will see what surrounds
my heart, the love that wants to seep through the
open door.

ESCAPE-BREAK THROUGH-REACH OUT-STRETCH
FORTH-Open the door, let your love spring forth-no
drawing back-no hiding

Open The Door-

The Door of Love-

Love Conquers All.

ALL WILL COME

Stop by here and see what I am doing, see what
I am exploring. My mind is wondering, I wish
and I dream of all my accomplishments-but
much more I desire-All Will Come.

It's not too late to reach the top-never stop-
All will Come-too soon too late-make it happen
for you-for me-for the world to see-All Will Come.

Now is the time to explore your mind-set your
goals-young or old-It's never to late to achieve
life's mysteries-search for them-don't give up-It's
here, it's there, for you to see-work hard-focus
on your dream-and never let go-All Will Come.

TIMELESS-TIME

Time is Timeless
Timeless Time
No beginning
No end.
No matter which way you go;
what you see-what you know
Far-Too-Far-Not Far Enough
Time-Timeless
Can't see; can't Feel-No that
it is there-always-never goes
anywhere
Stays in place-isn't so-can't
go-won't let go-nowhere-
Time.

Hurry, Get It
Wrap it around you like a
band tight-Knock, Open, Where
did it go-Leaks out-seeps out
Drips to no end.

Wasting your time-not worth a
dime-every moment counts-can't
reach-have to get it-obtain it-Now
this moment.

Time what is it-It comes and goes;
comes-comes again.

Don-t waste your time
Don't waste mine
Time is, time was-time will come again
No beginning-No Ending

Time-Less-Time-More
Time-Not Enough-More Than Enough

USE IT-TIME

TODAY-TOMORROW

Today is the day to begin afresh-what was once
started yesterday-tomorrow will complete every
angle of your life.

Today you will see what you will do-what you will
become-the greatness of who you are today, not
yesterday-but tomorrow.

Today you will look up-see the strength of your
mind-not yesterday, but tomorrow-your
accomplishments, your goals, your desires have
come-today, not yesterday-but tomorrow.

Today reach and grab hold of all that's yours-not
yesterday-tomorrow.

You will be life's brightness-this universe accepts
you, your hopes, your dreams, your talents

Strength is yours, today, yesterday, tomorrow-
tomorrow today=Reach Up-Reach Out-It's yours
today.

Your Mind-Is your strength of Tomorrow---

YOUR DREAM.

FREE TO SPEAK

I am Free-Free at last-like a bird that flies
through the air-at any time; day or night-night
or day. No one is disturbed by the sounds of
a bird.

Is it free to speak its own language as it pleases?
It is free-I am free to speak. My voice cries out
and rings throughout the universe;

AMERICA I AM FREE

DIE TO LIVE

Oh how it hurts-to-die-to live.

The outer self struggles, fights, cry to hold on-we
must die to selfishness, bitterness, anger,
unforgiving-light must shine; through inner
strength will blossom-love will come forth, laughter
will fill the air-As We Die To Live.

We must die to self-negative thoughts no more;
the fighting, the struggle will end as we search inside
the walls of our mind.

The rain, the storm, strong winds will exhale as we go
inside to find what is-we can give all to life-As We Die
To Live.

MAP OF LIFE

Zig-Zag-side-to-side-up-down-the
Map of Life.

Oceans, rivers, floods, streams-a time to go-a time
to stop-a time to move or not-when, how, where
what, which road do I take-where do I go,
How can I see-my future is there, here, where-stand
still-do I, should I-could I-let this Map of Life stop,
no-of course not.

I will travel this road and will do what my mind is
told-take commands and learn from demands;

Taking nothing, taking all, achieving the goals,
the gold of life that offers me fullness, fulfillment,
satisfaction, settlement, expansion.

The map of your life-your life the map-the stories
it tells-for you, for me, for the world to see-travel it,
explore it-take hold and never let go-

YOUR MAP OF LIFE

LET IT BE

My mind says to dislike you; hold a grudge
against you, but my heart says to keep loving
you over and over again.

You want me to hate you, distaste you, but my
heart says I can't. I do not understand
my heart; only God knows that part. The thoughts
to dislike you sometimes distracts my life. I must
go on and continue to love you.

I can only be set free by letting you go; never
understanding why you did this to me. You were
not free to love or to care, so how can I hate you;
distaste you and not really care.

You need someone to love you.

WHY NOT LET IT BE ME

HOLINESS

The Psalmist wrote "Holiness, that's what I long for."

Our spirit desires to live a life of holiness-
pureness. Is this always possible? I
say yes-I say no.

We are merely human beings and so
imperfect too. We try to live a holy life;
doing our best; trying not to make a mess
of our lives.

The flesh is very weak and the world seems
to be in control; but we have to know and
be determined to live this life of

HOLINESS

Now, we cannot judge one another by what
they say or do. If it wasn't for the Grace of
God; you would do just what they do.

There is hope for everyone that they can
start afresh-anew again.

GOD IS A GIVING GOD-He knows and
understands. You will have to make a
choice for God never demands. He just
wants us to live a holy life and obey His
commands.

GOD LOVES YOU

FALLEN IN LOVE

The song writer wrote and song this song:

FALLEN IN LOVE WITH JESUS WAS THE
BEST THING I'VE EVER DONE.

When you fall in love with Jesus, you will
have fallen in love with yourself. You will
not depend on someone else loving you.
He will give you all the love you need; He
will do it all for you-others' love toward you can
sometimes change.

I say that, to say this. Without love, it is
impossible to please God-for God is Love.
The world cannot see what it means to thee
to put God first in their lives. If only they knew
what God could do, they would never be the same;

THEIR LIVES WOULD CHANGE FOREVER

Love, joy and peace sustains you; though life is
the same; you have changed-you will never be the
same.

YOU HAVE FALLEN IN LOVE WITH JESUS

FREEDOM

Every city, every town, every state; the Nation.
Loud and soft, high and low, we come together
in unity to sing those words that we all know.

GOD BLESS ANERICA

Now, let's come together in everything we do;
speak our minds about issues that are fresh
and new.

VICTORY FOR US IS HERE

We can do this. We are free-people of every
color. It doesn't matter where we come from,
but it matters where we are going. We are free
to speak, to pray, to have our say.

THIS IS AMERICA

Stop being stubborn, thinking you are always
right. Let's come together and fight for the
things that are right.

We need to succeed; we need to stay free;
no bondage here; no where.

THIS IS AMERICA

FLY FREE AS A BIRD

Where did she come from; hiding away from me?
From everyone she sees? She knows where I am,
but I cannot find her; hiding in a tree or in a cave
or on top of the roof top; sometimes in the light,
sometimes in the dark.

Where are you My Friend?
I live deep within your spirit.

When will I be free? When life departs from
me into the grave-I rest my soul-then I will be
set free from all of this misery.

Now is not the time, for God has a special place
for me-HERE

Now spring forth and fly like a bird; now is your
time; your time has come for you to reach out;
go deep within-God is calling you to that place.

NOW REST AND FLY HIGH AND SEE

PEACE RETURN

WHY ARE YOU CRYING

Hold me close to you; sooth me now.
Your meekness, your kindness, your
love is all I need. Why are you crying?
I am hear to comfort you.

The tears run down your little face and
it makes me want to cry too, but I
know I have to be strong for you.

IT IS ALRIGHT TO CRY

Do you want to tell me now? Why
you are crying so much? You are not
the only one; look across from you;
see, that little boy and little girl, they
are crying too. While running down the
hill, they tripped over one another. Mommy
comes running over to wipe their tears away.

She doesn't say; why are you crying? She
sees the pain on their faces and kisses the
tears away. She begins to say; don't worry
I know why you are crying today.

Don't cry any more; mommy is here to
wipe away your tears.

ALWAYS

CAN YOU

You can do it; you just don't want to.
You're use to everybody doing it for
you.

GET REAL-life does not cater to
you; you cater to life.

You don't wait for life to change-
you make a change for yourself in
life-Nobody is going to do it for
you-NO MORE

Can you change your course of
life, the direction in which you are
going? Yes, you can; stop feeling
sorry for yourself and-MOVE ON.

You were born to live; make something
out of yourself; for me, for others
to see.

Stop taking others things; robbing from
them. Get a job-START OVER

Life begins with you. I think you can
make it; you can do it.

PEACE

MY HOUSE IS A MESS

On the inside.
On the outside
Is your house a mess?
Do you know where you are going?

Are you confused too; not knowing
what to do.

YOUR HOUSE IS A MESS THAT'S WHY

Throw out that junk; that baggage too.
Now you can move around. Stop
holding bitterness, hatred and blame
every time things don't go your way.

YOUR HOUSE IS A MESS

Clean it up-place it with love and
see the difference. Inside and out
you will shine among the best-your
love will come seeping through. All
that mess that was once in your house
is now no more.

NOW LIVE ON

BEHIND CLOSED DOORS

So many of us live behind closed doors;
can't come out; afraid to come out;
won't come out.

Fear has taken a hold of you; who did
that to you? Your life is engulfed in fear.

You won't go to the mailbox; you won't
step outside; the sunshine awaits you-
you hide

BEHIND CLOSED DOORS

Let me help you escape those fears
that have been embedded into your
brain for so long. Let me help you
love yourself again;

IT CAN BEGIN NOW

There is no life for you behind those
closed doors-emptiness and loneliness,
that can all disappear. Let me help
you love yourself again.

Once you escape and smell that fresh
air; you will breath life again; now outside
those doors.

LET ME HELP YOU LIVE AGAIN

GO AWAY

You can't stay here anymore-you are pulling
me down to the ground;

YOU HAVE TO GO AWAY

Your bad habits, your ugly ways has
caused me too much misery, pain
and heartache and you have no desire
to change.

GO AWAY YOU CAN'T STAY HERE ANYMORE

You keep hiding behind me thinking every-
thing is ok.; wanting to have your way; but I
know the real deal.

You only have one life to live; don't you think
it is time to change. Now consider how worth-
while it is to you to move forward, to enjoy the
good things this life has to offer you.

You can't come back this time to stay. I
must be strong and let you go-

GO AWAY TO FIND YOURSELF

MY HEART SAYS YES

I love you from the bottom of my heart.
Your warmth, your closeness captures
my soul. Where did you come from?
No one really knows.

You have no beginning.
You have no ending.

You have always been forever
present. My heart did not love
you then; but you knew way back
then the closeness we would have
one day; loving one another in such
a special way.

Now, I can't even imagine not loving
you. You always loved me from the
beginning of time; waiting patiently for
me to love you back. Your love never
fails;

YOU LOVE ME UNCONDITIONALLY

I only put my faith in you; no man
can do what you can do for me;

LOVING ME LIKE THIS

You caress me; you hold me tight
in your arms; what peace I feel just
knowing you are there. Your touch
means so much to me

MY HEART KEEPS SAYING YES

MAYBE YES MAYBE NO

Come on, every day it's the same thing you do;
fooling around, pondering about what to do.

MAYBE YES/MAYBE NO

Stop wasting my time-your time-trying to
decide what step to make-what path to
take. One minute you want to take the
road that points North; other times the
one that points South. Your mind is
so confused. I wish you would make a
decision on what you want to do

YOUR TIME IS WASTING AWAY

Just say no-just say yes-but praying
for God's direction is the best.

You have a choice to make; where is
your life going-nowhere, you're just sitting
around expecting someone to do it for
you.

I cannot make life choices for you, but
I can encourage you to stop saying
Maybe Yes or Maybe No; and move on
with your life.

This is my last chance to counsel you.
I have to move on to help someone new,
Yes or no, no; yes

Your mind is playing tricks on you; now the
game of your mind is over for you. This is
your life of accomplishments.

JUST SAY YES

IT'S SLIPPERY OUT HERE

Help me I am sliding. I keep trying
to go uphill, but life keeps pulling
me down-deep in despair.

Life is like a sliding board; going up
then coming down; but when we reach
the bottom, we have another chance
to reach the top-AGAIN

Picking yourself up is the key word here.
It's not always easy to start over again.
It can be very hard at times; depression
comes and takes over our mind so that
we can't make there-to the place God
has for us.

Our whole life is like a sliding board;
slippery and wet; tears falling at times; but
the key word here is that.

YOU CAN BEGIN AGAIN

Just say in your mind; I am going to
try again and live to see my life begin-
fresh-new;

MY LIFE

There is happiness; peace, love and joy
that dwells inside of me.

THANK YOU LORD FOR HELPING ME
THROUGH THIS SLIPPERY ROAD OF LIFE

I'M STILL HERE

Say to yourself; I am still here

You have made it thus far and you
have far to go-travelling this road
call "LIFE"

YOU ARE STILL HERE

I know you have been abused,
sexually, physically, emotionally too.
You shed many tears; closed yourself
behind closed doors; lived in a closet
for so long. Much of you have been lost
because of your past, your pain, your
hurt; all of your suffering.

Remember this one thing, no matter what
hardships life brings, you made it through
the toughest experiences.

You are a special human being; let no one
crush you again. Your life is in God's hands;
and He loves you so much-I love you too.

YOU ARE STILL HERE

I AM LIVING AGAIN

I was alive; doing, going about my everyday tasks;
thinking about caring for everybody else; making
sure all their needs were met. I lost myself; where
did I go? I didn't intend to stop living; forgetting about
myself and stop doing-enjoying what life has to
offer me.

I am special too, so here I am sitting, wondering
what to do-I feel selfish if I don't only take care
of you.

I have to change and realize too, that I must live
again. This talent that God gave me; birthed
inside of me, has laid here untouched for too long-

LIFE BEGINS FOR ME NOW

I am filling my dreams

NOW I AM LIVING

MY GIFT TO YOU

It's not in a box wrapped with beautiful paper
and a great big bow.

MY GIFT TO YOU

My gift to you is not small or large-thin
or wide to sit on the shelf of your home.
If it is not toys, or clothes or accessories,
What can it be?

MY GIFT TO YOU

It's a gift you will always remember; rather
young or old; my legacy I leave to you. My
compassion, my love I give to you forever.

I listen to you; I give my advice; I realize
that I am not always right; but MY GIFT
TO YOU is forever;

LOVING YOU UNTIL DEATH US PART-MY CHILD

WHEN I PRAY

My Father which Art in Heaven, hallow be
your name; thy kingdom come in my life
today.

When I pray, my words do not always
say what my heart is feeling. I know for
sure, without a doubt, my faith can move
the hand of God; my Daddy; my Father
from above.

He knows what I need; he knows my
desires; He feels my hurt, my pain; but

WHEN I PRAY

His ears are forever open to hear my voice;
to thank Him for a fresh new day; giving me
a chance to connect with Him; to communicate
with Him

WHEN I PRAY

He has so many good things for me. I
wouldn't dare not pray and miss that opportunity
to receive His joy and love. I feel My Father's
arms around me, knowing He is always there.

WHEN I PRAY

LIFT UP YOUR HEAD

Why are you downcast?
Why are you sad?
Why are you feeling lonely?
as if no one cares?

I know it is not easy to always snap
out of it. The pain is so great, but
remember someone cares. He will
be there to hold you tight and wipe
away your tears,

MY GOD

That hole of emptiness will still be
there for awhile, but you will

LIFT UP YOUR HEAD AGAIN

The Psalmist wrote:

"Lift Up Your Head oh you gates and
be lifted up ye everlasting doors, and
the King of Glory shall come in. Who
is this King of Glory? He is strong and
mighty-mighty in battle. Now pause and
think about that

YOU WILL LIFT UP YOUR HEAD AGAIN

THE SOIL THE DIRT

I lay and wait to smell and feel the leaves
of different colors. I am the soil, the dust
of the earth. I help the flowers to grow and
the trees to bloom full forever.

Man was formed from me. Breath of
Life came inside of me from God.

You were birthed from me and will
return to me, but while you are here,
breath the Life of Breath inside of me,

LIVE

Do all that God called you to do. Care
about the people you meet. Your joy and
your peace will return-then you feel that
fulfillment-that missing piece inside of you
again.

THE BREATH OF LIFE

that God put inside of you. There is a purpose
for you; now don't you forget; Let God Do It-Serve
Him; Your Joy, Your Peace Will Come.

JUST BREATH

THANK YOU GOD

Thank you God for loving me; you sent your
only son to die for me-so I can love you;
serve you-BE FREE.

Free inside to express openly how I can
minister to others so they can have life
eternally. Only accepting you into my
heart can my life be free.

It is so easy to love you. You ask so
little of us. You want the best for us.
Trusting you and believing what we hear
and read is true-The Word of God can really
set you free. Remember this too; it is
so important to you; He sent His son to
die that you can have life more abundantly
and live life in eternity.

All you ask from all of us is to love you;
obey your commands; believe that you are
real. As we put our lives into your hands;
to guide us protect us, love us, no matter
what we do-you love us unconditionally.

No one can love us the way you do. I
wish people would understand that your
love is true-FOREVER LASTING.

Thank you Lord for choosing me to be able
to love you freely;

THAT'S THE GREATEST GIFT OF ALL

THANK YOU LORD< AGAIN

BE CAREFUL

Don't step over me. Who do you think you
are? Are you aware of whom I am?

Be careful what you say about me; what
you do to me today; Just don't step over
me.

You act as though I don't exist. You try to
wipe me out with your strong words again
today; trying to destroy me; breaking me down
emotionally.

Be careful what you do and say; stepping over
me each day. You think you can destroy me,
crush me to the ground. You are wrong; you
are only making me strong.

Each time you take that step to mentally destroy
me; making me a mess inside; the words inside
of me say.

BE CAREFUL WHAT YOU DO TO ME.

You will go under and I will arise and tell others-
LOOK-SEE, I was once under your control but
now;

I RISE

BE CAREFUL.

STEP BY STEP

It's not hard
Take one step at a time and
you will eventually get there.

Don't skip a step, don't turn
the wrong way or get lost on the
highway call life.

Don't be afraid. You will get what
life has laid out for you. Don't skip
a step; just walk patiently; knowing and
being assured that you will make progress-
taking the road of success;

FREEDOM TO EXPLORE

Don't jump in front of what lies ahead of
you. You will come to the end where your
journey begins.

SUCCESS ONLY COMES THAT WAY

STEP BY STEP

CAN ANYBODY HEAR

Hello, can anybody here me down here. I feel
you walking, running, and jumping on top of my head.
I am so strong, you can't crush me.

Can you hear me say I am determined to succeed?
To proceed, to go forth in life. You keep
stomping on top of me-trying to keep me from
having the victory. Don't you know, I will rise-can
rise from underneath your feet. You cannot chase
me away-. I am here to stay-successful and strong,
determined too, to make it.

I have a voice; can you hear me-LISTEN-I can tell
you more about life then you can see.

I AM SUCCESSFUL

TAKE ME UP

Up, Up, away I go to a place of quietness, serenity,
joy and peace. The light of life has taken me up
to be with thee.

Why did it take so long for you to take hold of
Me? to allow me to be with you in eternity.
What? It isn't time yet?

In my mind I am going up and away, but my
body is down here to stay; until you call me home.

IT'S ISN'T MY TIME YET

Will it be today that you take me away to be with
you forever-we never know the hour or the day.

I won't go astray. I will stay close to you and
obey; knowing one day I will live with you forever.

I TRUST IN YOU TO RAPTURE ME UP ONE DAY

MY CHILD YOUR CHILD

Who's that little boy? That little girl swinging on
the swings? I don't know who they are; but it could
be my child. I can't go near to really see; is that
my child or your child or could it be another.

It doesn't really matter; we can see from afar that
each child is the same; watching them both having
fun and playing all kinds of games; my child, your
child.

They fall down.
They get up.
They both share tears.
They both go back and play.

So what's the difference between each child? They
are both enjoying life; laughing, playing and
having fun. One is my child. One is your child. They
are both special to me.

LOVE THEM BOTH

MOMMY'S DADDY'S

Mommy, daddy, mommy's, daddy's girl-
mommy's, daddy's baby; mommy's
daddy's girl.

All grown up; I learned so much, being
your little girl. Your hugs; your kisses;
you held me so tight. When I was afraid
at night, who tucked me in so tight; wrapped
her body close to mine-MY MOMMY.

My daddy wasn't always there; he worked so
hard to provide for us; he was a top notch chef.
He really cared and loved me so much giving
me the best things that life could offer a little
girl.

I didn't know how blessed I was but as I look
back and see, I lived a life of victory. I never
wanted for nothing at all, he gave me the best
life could offer.

HIS LOVE

I'll never forget-to me-you were

THE BEST MOMMY AND DADDY

could have.

I MISS YOU BOTH

FRESHNESS

I can breathe again.
I was all stuffed up; blocked
up in this cage inside of me.

Open Up-Let the fresh air in
so I can breathe again. I can see;
I can hear I can feel all the wonderful,
beautiful things that exist inside of me.

I can appreciate what God has given me.
I am so grateful that the love God has
placed in me, can now flow freely. I
can breathe this in; breathe it out.

THE FRESHNESS OF LIFE

Come take this journey with me

THE BREATH OF LIFE

SLOW DOWN

Slow down; why are you racing like that; you won't
go no farther than that; travelling with the thoughts
that are racing in your mind.

SLOW DOWN

Give it to God; all those thoughts that keep you
awake at night; throughout your day. If you keep
going this way, there will be no more thoughts
travelling your way. Your mind will become dead,
no matter how much you try; the thoughts of your
mind will die.

YOU DIDN'T LET GO

I'm giving you another chance to follow the path
that I have for you. Just stop travelling through
your mind all those thoughts; trying to figure it
out. It's in God's hands.

JUST SLOW DOWN

MY MOTHER

My mother had me in her change of life; she was
the oldest.

I didn't understand why she stayed inside the
house, cooking, cleaning and sewing. She was
always willing to hold me tight against her breast;
keeping me safe with a freshness and her beauty
to love me.

MY MOTHER

We had the best clothes to wear and the best
food to eat, all cooked by my mother. Even
though my dad went to work as a chef each day'
coming home late; it didn't matter.

SHE KEPT LOVING ME

She always said I lived my life when I was younger;
now I am a mother-THE OLDEST.

She was always home for me; morning, noon and
night; never leaving me alone. As I look back, I don't
think she was free; she gave up her life to live the
life as a mother-THE OLDEST

Other mothers went out at night-took their flight-
partying. My friends had no one to hold them.

Even though she was unable to move around like
some of the others; she was so special to me; she
was THE GREATEST.

I followed her path and had my last in my change of
life; I was also the oldest mother.

I am glad I had the oldest mother. I learned from her
how to be the same

ARMY BOOTS

My feet are warm protecting me from the storms
of life. I cannot feel the cold even though I know
it really snowed. Can you feel the cold when you
walk in the rain or climb those muddy roads?

You are fighting so that we can be free

YOU WEAR THOSE ARMY BOOTS

We know you will come home wearing those
same army boots; from a land of bondage to
a land that is free. You have helped us to live
free from the enemy.

With you away, we can live free, not being afraid
of another attack from that enemy.

WE APPRECIATE YOU

You keep those boots on; you are so strong to
be willing to fight on foreign soil to set us free.

YOU FIGHT ON ANOTHER'S TERRITORY

Those army boots have fought many wars;
risking their lives to conqueror the battle'

SETTING AMERICA FREE

I feel safe.

I feel protected.

THANK YOU MY FRIEND

HIDING

Where did she come from? She is hiding away from
me; from everyone she sees. She knows where
I am, but I cannot find her; hiding in a tree or in a
cave, maybe under a rock or bark;

ALWAYS IN THE DARK

Come forth little one. You are so precious
to me. You don't have to keep hiding your
beautiful self from thee.

ALWAYS IN THE DARK

We can see you and you can feel the warmth,
your love, swing forth. In the light, in the dark;
wherever you are; you cannot hide no more.

She will come out to take her life back to be
free;

RETURN TO HER PEACE

LAST

Don't you know that this won't last? This too
shall pass. This will end; a new beginning
has begun; a chance has come again for you

A NEW DAY

Each day comes a new beginning of that day-
that day will go away; won't last; you're given
a chance again to begin afresh.

The last is lost forever gone from your mind-
your heart. last, finally, the beginning has
begun for you.

Don't share tears, regrets no more-The lost is
the last-you have found the new-THE BEGINNING.
Last night was the end; the morning is the beginning
of your life again.

ONCE AGAIN IT HAS COME

WHAT HAPPENED?

What Happened?

I finally realized that you are the same. You
say one thing but do another; you speak from
your mind and not from your heart-

WHAT HAPPENED TO YOU?

You say I am not like the others; just give
me a chance to prove to you that I am a
real man.

WHAT HAPPENED?

You say trust me. I'm honest, trustworthy and real,
give me another chance still-I'll show you, I really
will-and you asked me

WHAT HAPPENED?

Well, I tell you; I keep waiting for you to change,
but you continue to play games with my mind.

You know what; I won't allow you to make me change
to become someone I'm not. I will continue to be whom
I am; loving, trustworthy, honest and true.

I begin to say to myself; No, men are not at all the
same-some are honest, loving and trustworthy too-Now

WHAT HAPPENED TO YOU?

It's time to make a change. I assure you of this one thing;

I AM WHAT'S HAPPENING

I AM COMING OUT

I lay and wait too smell and feel food of
different colors. Cover me up; if you do not
the little ones will crawl all over me. Inside
of me they eat everything and leave me empty
to be disposed of.

What is it that is doing this to me? I was not
born this way-disease go away. Go away
depression, oppression and doubt; for I am
coming out. You no longer have to cover me
up from these little pests that eat inside of me.

I HAVE COME OUT AGAIN

To smell, to feel, to enjoy, to love everything
of different colors.

PEACE

The cry of a baby; the screams of children
playing; the laughter from games while playing;
the sound of birds chirping; the noise of a dog
barking.

IS THAT PEACE?

We think of peace as stillness, quietness,
a calmness inside of us.

The life of a baby crying is peace-LIFE
LIFE brings much peace. Even in pain,
sufferings and trials, lies peace inside of
thee. It is always there but we cannot always
see because of life's tragedies-there still lies
peace inside-GOD'S PEACE.

The joy comes when you here life springing
forth from that child at play; laughing, jumping,
swinging, running. Just stop and look in the
face of that child-Today is Life-Today is Peace.

A mother reading.
A grandmother sleeping
A father laughing
A grandfather pondering; Is Peace.

Life gives more hope, more joy, more peace.

Peace comes to all, only in different ways; on
different days, but; peace still comes-will come
Just Believe; It shall be yours again-again today.

SHARING

They just don't know what you have done for me,
but I know in my heart and I do believe that the
world will know what you will do for me-Greater
things are about to come.

I will share with the world the gift God has given
me, so that some else's life can be set totally
free. They will surely know and be assured-only
you God can love them unconditionally; you are
always there; you have been there for me all of
the time.

He wants you to know that he really cares and
wants to share your life with you; together, entwined.

My life has now been set free.

Let Him share with you; giving you the freedom to
share with others too.

HELP TO SET SOMEELSE'S LIFE FREE
YOU'RE ALWAYS THE SAME

When I call you, you are always there; you never
change. You never get tired of listening to my voice;
today, tomorrow, you are always the same-caring,
loving, compassionate and true; you guide my life
each day making it afresh and anew. I grab hold of
what you have to say-revealing something new and
wonderful; my prayer has been answered.

In my darkest hour, you are there-God of the Universe;
I know you really care about me. Peace that passed all
understanding; joy unspeakable-My God; My Love; you
are always there-you never change.

You understand my every need-you are the one that
provides for me-man cannot ever do what you have
already done for me-THEY CHANGE-

YOU ARE ALWAYS THE SAME-MY GOD

DEEPNESS

How deep, is that hole you have
dug for yourself? Each day you fill it up
with junk that doesn't matter; things that
won't last; people who care less; to them
nothing matters what you are going through.

Stop allowing that hole in your heart to be
filled with sympathy-despair-hopelessness.
What's done, is done; what's gone, is gone;
can't come back. Now cover that hole and
never go back to see how deep or how steep
it has become.

It's time to heal-go forward still, because life
has just begun for you.

Now promise yourself, no more sympathy
or pity; wanting-waiting for someone to
love thee. Remember this one thing, God's
love for you will never change.

Permanent Peace, Permanent Joy, Permanent
Love forever.

A DEEP LOVE-FOR YOU

THESE VOICES

My voices, your voice, we all have this voice
deep inside of us, crying out to come forth
from us; just this tiny little voice.

What is this small voice saying to us; a
whisper inside, don't cry, everything will be
alright. This is just your season-to reason and
think what today will bring to your life again;
beauty, hope, experience that will help you
grow-there is no end to that voice that speaks
inside.

What is speaking unto you? All your dreams,
your visions; what you can do in this life now-
Accomplish what that little voice is telling you-

*SPEAK IT OUT-DO IT TODAY-IT IS NEVER
TOO LATE-NOW IS YOUR TIME*

THOSE SOUNDS

I hear the sounds inside of you; listen don't
you hear them too.

What is that sound I hear? Is it ringing louder
inside my ear? My mind, my heart says; listen
to what God is saying to you; that sweet, sweet
sound of victory-ringing-softness, warmth, love
holding you. Don't let go. Let the sounds of
laughter flow. Let the tears of joy come streaming
down your face.

Rescue me; rescue me- Lead the way for me
today,

TO THE LAND OF PROMISE

TO THE LAND OF FREEDOM

TO MY HOME

WHAT'S IN THAT MIRROR

Stop trying to change yourself-what's
in the mirror is what God gave you
You can see the outside, now examine
the inside-YOUR HEART

Inner beauty outweighs outer beauty;
you are passing life's opportunities
worrying about what you look like
on the outside; comparing yourself
to others.

WHAT DO YOU SEE IN THAT MIRROR?

Oh, you are so beautiful; you must begin
to see what God has given you. You are
so beautiful on the inside-YOUR HEART

Don't destroy yourself trying to be someone
else-YOU ARE BEAUTIFUL

You don't see what I see. I see beauty that
lies deep within; a heart that loves; a giving
heart. Do us a favor and check yourself out
once more.

Let that mirror reflect the beauty inside of you.

DON'T CHANGE A THING

YOU'RE ALWAYS THE SAME

When I call you, you are always there; you never
change. You never get tired of listening to my voice;
today, tomorrow, you are always the same-caring,
loving, compassionate and true; you guide my life
each day making it afresh and anew. I grab hold of
what you have to say-revealing something new and
wonderful; my prayer has been answered.

In my darkest hour, you are there-God of the Universe;
I know you really care about me. Peace that passed all
understanding; joy unspeakable-My God; My Love; you
are always there-you never change.

You understand my every need-you are the one that
provides for me-man cannot ever do what you have
already done for me

THEY CHANGE-

YOU ARE ALWAYS THE SAME-MY GOD

WHERE DID SHE COME FROM

Where did she come from? Hiding away from
me, from everyone she sees.

Where are you my friend? I live deep within
your spirit.

When will I be free? When life departs from
me into the grave; I rest my soul; then I am
set free from all of this misery.

No, now is not the time. God has a special
place for me

HERE

Now spring forth; come on out now; the time
has come; your destiny. God is calling you to
that place

NOW REST AND SEE

PEACE RETURNS

Biography

As the youngest daughter of Gertrude and Julius Jones, I was born and raised in n upstate New York, n the City of Albany on Oct. 27, 1948. My dad was a chef and catered many of Governor Rockefeller's parties and functions. My mother was a wonderful homemaker and a fantastic cook.

I graduated from Albany High School n 1966 and Albany Business College in 1968. My first professional job as a legal secretary was with the law firm of Ainsworth, Sullivan, Tracey and Knauf. Upon leaving that position, I became a Court Reporter for Newburgh City Court in Newburgh, New York; under Judge McDowell. I also worked for BM Corporation in Albany and later transferred to IBM in Trenton, Jersey. Before coming home to raise my three sons, I worked for the Appellate Division State of New Jersey; also in Trenton.

My oldest son was a prosecutor for five years with the Salem County Court system in Salem, New Jersey but is now presently employed as an attorney for the law firm of Helmer, Paul, Conley and Kasselman of Haddon Heights, New Jersey. My second son is a Culinary Arts Teacher for Burlington County Institute of Technology in Westampton Township, New Jersey. He also has a very prosperous catering business.

My youngest son is an assistant supervisor for Occupational Training Center in Mount Holly, New Jersey and is also a full time student Burlington County College in Pemberton, New Jersey; majoring in Psychology.

My purpose and fulfillments are to continue feeding hungry children and families, which I will continue to do by purchasing grocery gift cards. Much of my proceeds from this book will go to that cause.

ℬ ℭ

Breinigsville, PA USA
01 March 2011
256653BV00001B/8/P